Thoughts Through the Process

Desha Anthony

Photographer: Miles Jay Robinson

AuthorHouse™
1663 Liberty Drive
Bloomington, IN 47403
www.authorhouse.com
Phone: 1 (800) 839-8640

This book is printed on acid-free paper.

ISBN: 978-1-7283-4324-2 (sc)
ISBN: 978-1-7283-4323-5 (e)

Print information available on the last page.

Published by AuthorHouse 01/23/2020

authorHOUSE®

I hope when you read these pages you're able to reflect on your journey, know where you are, appreciate it and grow from there.

Know GOD will never Leave or Forsake You.

People are people,
They make mistakes,
They disappoint others,
People hurt people.
Though we know this, we still choose to love them

Even when we are the ones
That are getting hurt, or feeling less than because of another person,
We still choose to love them.

Even when they act like they don't care,
And act like they don't need us,
We still just want to be there,
We think, maybe one day they'll treat us good,
Maybe one day they'll show that they care and show affection
Maybe one day they'll change

We get disappointed
We get our hopes up thinking someone is going to change
We tend to forget that people are stuck in their own ways,
We tend to forget that people ultimately think of themselves,

People are selfish.
They can say they love somebody
and not care if they are happy or not
They don't care if they cry
They don't care if they don't feel wanted

People seem to contradict themselves
when they say the words
I love you

Maybe they just don't know what love is,
Or how to love.

People are funny,
Situations are funny,
Life is funny.
Sometimes you have to just laugh.

In the end,
everything works out
everything will fall in to place,
everything will be okay.

You just have to get through the day
One step at a time.
One task at a time.

Everything works out for the greater good and everything happens for a
reason.

Who am I trying to convince?
The pages or myself?

Are people really who they say they are?

Does everyone put on a fake smile or just a fake face to help them tolerate what happens during a regular day?

Is life that hard?

Do people know who they really are? or do they just have an idea and roll with it?

The thorns are what creates the beauty not the flower.

Letter to myself.

You are more than what you believe yourself to be. You are not stuck, you ae always moving forward.

You are not ugly you are beautiful, inside and out.

Give life a chance, everyone will not hurt you. Give people a chance, you need human interaction, at this point in your life you're not good at being alone.

You are joy.
You are laughter.
You are happiness.

Though you have a wall up, allow yourself to be who you truly are.

You could light up a room when you walk in, and your smile is contagious. Your laugh makes people happy, but you don't laugh a lot anymore.

You feel as if you're so deep in a hole that you can't get out but you're not alone.

Break your walls down but keep your feelings guarded. Have discernment, everyone is not who they say they are.

Pray. A prayer works miracles.
You're going to be okay. Everything will be okay. Everything you need you will have, everything that stands in your way will be removed.
I promise.

Love, Desha.

You can find light in a dark place,
although the memories are hard to erase.
The way someone treats you, sticks in your head,
You don't see their face you see their actions instead

Is that true?
Do people become a new person to you?
Do you let their actions determine who they are?
Have you ever let it go that far?

People are people.
We make mistakes.
We don't understand our own pace.

The rate our mouth is moving,
we can't comprehend.
The words that come out,
There is no end.
They stay in our head if they're not expressed.
They continuously repeat and leave you stressed.

We let the words out,
With little thought or none.
When we get a reaction the test has begun.

Can we be kind after hearing what we don't want to hear?

Can we handle millions of things thrown at us at the end of the year?

Is it possible to find light in a dark place?

Is it possible for you to separate actions from a face?

Journal Entry:

*I'd rather be in a state of confusion than a place of conclusion
just because I'm scared of what's going to come next how I'm going to
feel.
Or how I'm going to react if things change.
or how I'll react if things
don't change.
I can't tell if I'm more afraid of the change or the lack of it.
Sometimes I keep myself in these situations and I want to get out of it
but I'm never 100% sure,
the uncertainty drives me insane.*

That's the problem, the uncertainty,
I don't deal with it well.
I don't like putting my all into something that may or may not work out
I'm afraid of wasting my time and while knowing that I could avoid
being hurt,
But I don't avoid it.

These tears trickle down my cheeks
at the same pace the rain falls from the sky on a stormy day.

But I'm tired of crying,
I'm tired of the pain.
I'm tired of the knots that stay in my stomach
I'm tired of all the thoughts that stay in my head.

Stop avoiding things,
Ease your mind.

Learn to love yourself
before focusing on giving all your love to another being.
Make yourself happy first.

Face you fear.
Change isn't always a bad thing
Don't be afraid to be alone
You are never really alone.

Joshua 1:9

Be strong and courageous
Do not be afraid
Do not be discouraged
For the Lord your God will be with you wherever you go.

Through darkness I see light,
even though it's kind of hard to reach,
sometimes do you ever.
well hopefully,
no one is reading this soon.

But do you ever just wonder if people really care as much as they say
they do?
Or if this life is so worth living that people just continue to deal with
the pain over and over again.
That it's okay, well wont it be one day? Wont everything just work
together for good, it will that's what the Lord says.
Everything works together for good.
I want a reason, I want an actual purpose, I'm not sure that I have one.

Thorns show character.
The sharp points add to the beauty of the actual flower.
It shows us that beautiful things still have the potential to hurt,
but that doesn't take away the fact
the flower is still beautiful.

Allow yourself to Dream Big.

Don't Settle for Less.

Go slow if you want to climb fast.

New experiences take you places.

Be open in your next relationship.

If it is meant to be, you won't have to force anything.

1st Corinthians 13:4-7

Love is patient, love is kind.
It does not envy,
it does not boast
It is not proud.
It does not dishonor others,
It is not self -seeking,
It is not easily angered,
It keeps no record of wrongs.
Love does not delight in evil
but rejoices with the truth.

It always protects,
It always trusts,
It always hopes,
It always perseveres.

Lack of

Pink skies
Red moon
Inspiration everywhere,
But we chose not to look,
we choose not to care.

The world moves too fast.
People don't sit around and talk.
Feelings are too deep they'd rather just walk.
Walk away from the conversation,
Just to avoid a situation
Too many colors within ones' self
People would rather see less.

Wandering Wishing

Your body close to my body
Your fingers running down my spine
The whole time I'm sitting there,
wishing you were mine.
Wishing you were the one but what is the one?

Why can't there be a definition or an example,
of the perfect characteristics that meet our own
of the perfect person who isn't capable of turning my heart to stone.

Backtrack to you though,
I guess you'll mean more to me than you'll ever know.
I guess I might always be one step ahead.

I tend to fall hard, fall deep,
but at this point these may be words that I keep.
Maybe I'm wrong, maybe I'll get the explanation,
the one I've been waiting for, for so long.

Do you think I'm beautiful?
One day will you not?

Will I turn into your comfort zone?
Not your place of peace.
One day will I call you my own?
Will you be the better half of me?

Yes, we say words, we make plans too,
but what if we meet the inevitable?
What if my inevitable isn't you?
How do you feel about me?
What do you think of my mind?
How is it that we somehow connect?
How is it there's so little but so much time?

Time passes.
Time changes people's minds.
Time changes circumstances too.
Time heals but it hurts too.
The irony.

Due to circumstances,
I keep questions to myself.
Never to come to anyone else, not even you.
Not until the right time.

Not until I trust you completely.
I trust you but I'm hesitant with my heart.
I can't open up completely until I know.
Until I know, if you love me,
the way I love you.

Even though I love you, you couldn't be mine.
Not at this time
We both know right?
This isn't the right time.

I think this is my anxiety.
My thoughts taking over my head,
My worries causing my headaches,
My worries causing me to dread,
Dread the distance and time.

Your body close to my body
Your fingers running down my spine
the whole time I'm sitting there
wishing you were mine.

I think
I thought

I think I was in love with the idea of love,
the idea of always having someone there
just to avoid being alone.
The idea of loving someone and them loving me back.

I think I was in love with the image.
The title, the status I held.
Everyone had these expectations and visions
It's like I didn't want to fail

I think I was in love with the comfort.
the knowing I had a shoulder that would be there,
Someone cared, the knowing that someone cared.

This ball of fire,
It rises
I notice it
I'm aware
It's like trying to swallow a big pill.
I can control it sometimes I swear.

Pride.

Thank you so much
to the people that respect me.
I'm also so thankful
For the people that neglected me, that hurt me, that turned their back
on me.

I've came to the realization that the positive and negative aspects have
shaped me into the woman I am today.

-Desha Monet.

The floating
The flying
Better than barely surviving
The lack of sensing but actually sensing
But I wouldn't necessarily call it thriving

Thank you for the high,
Thank you for helping me with the pain in this life.
The pain running throughout my body.
Yes, the physical pain but the mental too.
You also give me a different perspective so thank you.
I see a different way, I see more.
I study people, observation to its core.
I'm always lucky enough to see and hear what others don't hear.
You amplify that gift for me.

Thank you for helping me to live a normal day.

Journal Entry:

Expression is good but is it still good when the one you're expressing yourself too isn't caring to listen or isn't caring enough to listen.

It's hard to express yourself to someone when you don't measure up to their level of importance.

Journal Entry:

You ever think about your future and realize at one point you thought you had it all figured out.

You had a plan, and everything was going according to plan and then everything stopped going right.

Now you have no idea what your future will look like.

That's where I'm at right now.

It's going to be okay.

Relationships are hard sometimes.
Falling in love with someone
forming expectations and attachments,
Trying to simply get two people to be with one another
seems impossible but it works.

However, what happens when it doesn't work?
The pain comes,
It rushes in like a dagger in flight
creating an empty feeling.

It forces you to,
deal with the option of letting go
or falling deeper with no assurance that the person you love will
catch you
when you fall
or know how to help you heal after you've picked yourself up again.

48

Love yourself because you are amazing.
Love yourself because God loves you
and he didn't make a mistake when he made you.

Life honestly seems pointless sometimes.
To constantly go through situations, trials, and tribulations.
to grow and get stronger.
What happens when we're tired of being strong?
When the situations and all the tribulations break us down.
We have to get up again,
We have to grow from what we just went through.

Life is a growing process.
It has many stages characterized by events that shape you into the person you're meant to be.

Grow
Gain wisdom
Be better
Not only for yourself but for the people around you.

You aren't allowed to waste your purpose.
Make an impact in people's lives.
Make people smile and want to live another day.

Everyone deserves a little light in their life.

Be the light.

I sit there quietly
as he fixates his eyes upon me.
I feel his gaze
Weighing on me, lingering, waiting.

I look up
Our eyes meet
For a split second
Before his head turns
And my eyes break away

Distracting
Distracted now.
Sitting there wondering,

Who are you?

The look, I noticed.

Will there soon be a day,
when I see those eyes,
those eyes,
that face,
again..

Wondering.

"Hey"
"..hey"

As you spoke, your voice seduced me.
Your lips pulled me in, however I focused,
on the words you said,
I made eye contact though in the physical,
I wanted to make contact,
To feel your brown skin on mine,
so close that the hairs on our skin
would stand for each other and intertwine.
Nevertheless, the conversation continued.

Phases.

No communication lead to a glance.
A glance lead to an introduction,
Followed by a conversation.

I didn't know what to think.
How is it so easy for people to..
open communication with someone and also
have open communication with them?

I did it.
I trusted so easy, I wanted to.
I wanted to believe that there was good people.
I wanted to believe that one of them was you.

I wanted to trust and believe the words coming from your lips.

You intrigued me,

physically and mentally.

You pleased me, my mind.

Attraction to the potential.

What could this be?

Do you trust people?
Do you give people a chance?
Do your form a judgement before taking a second glance?

What's your outlook on life?
What about your religious views?
Have you given up on believing in God because someone hurt you?

Do you respect women, people?
Do you respect yourself?
Do you have a giving heart?
Can you put people before yourself?

Do you think bad thoughts?
Do you speak your mind?
Do you react with emotions or take your time to use your mind?

Tell me about you.

Questions.

What do you want to know?

I ask myself,
why would I let this person enter my life?

Why do they deserve to be?

Will this person hurt me?
Will this person complement me?
Will this person destroy me?
Will this person build me up?

What impact will they have on my life?

Though I have no intention of falling for you, I wake the next day with your name between my lips.

I seen you as the faint light,
that shined
through my temporary cloud of darkness.

The sunflower in the rain.
You brightened a part of me that was dim,
just for a moment.

You were a mystery.
A random piece of a random puzzle.
A random door in a maze.
A random face in a crowd.
But you were a random face that stayed,
imprinted in my head.
As I went along during my day,
lyrics of a song reminded me of you.
As my day continued,
Your name was intertwined in my thoughts.
I didn't think twice,
I thought continuously.
You were a mystery.
I wanted to take away the impossibility,
of not having understanding.

MJR

You linger around the clouds that cover my eyes.

Recollection.
So many thoughts,
buried in the numb phase.

Opposed to when I think of you,
just a little less I ache,
from the pain that came before.

I need to restore before pouring myself into you.
Before my blood runs through your stream,
before your hand sends chills down my spine,
before my eyes get that gleam.

I need me.

That pain I felt,
It broke me.
left me shattered in pieces on the floor.
Struggling to fill the empty holes,
and I always went back for more,
never letting myself restore.

There was no time to heal,
no time to think about leaving.

In the back of my mind thoughts came,
but I forgot to feel anything.

I wish I could say your name doesn't,
pop up in my mind,
That your scent doesn't rise sometimes.
That the lyrics of a song don't remind me of you.
That I still don't think of you when I need someone to run too.

I will be proud when they day comes that I can look you in your face and
not feel anything negative towards you but content with the lessons you
taught me.

Don't get me attached to your branches and leaves
before letting my flowers bloom.

Don't get me attached,
to your branches and leaves,
before letting my flowers bloom.

Don't let me be consumed
with the thought of you.
Non intentional kindness.
Non intentional blindness.

It may be soon love,
Don't rush the cycle
of the stars and the moon.

Let my broken pieces come as one again.
Let my mountains move,
by my strength,
and my strength alone.

Wait until my flowers bloom.
Wait until my colors shine,
before you put effort and time into,
opening me up.

Petal by petal.
Fiber by fiber

My full exposure may cause you pain.
It's sad to say, it's too soon.
Too soon to expose.

Too soon to expose,
my heart to another being

To expose my deepest darkest pits

Too soon to trust another's intentions

To tell the difference between reality and myth.

My guards up, it terrifies me.
So genuine, the sincerity.

The first phase I see.

Though you're pulling my heartstrings,
wait for my spring.

You don't see me.
You think you see me.
You see my face, my smile occasionally.

How are you so certain,
I'd be the perfect "one" for you?

What if you don't like my attitude?
What if my emotions are too much for you?
What if my love isn't good enough for you?

How would you know?
You don't see me.
You see what you want to see,
for now.

Terrified of change but willing to make changes to benefit my mental state.

When I used to think about my future,
I thought about him.
About how our kids would be.
About our sincere moments.
About how happy we'd be.

However, there is no longer a We.
There is me.
There is me.

Though, I am not the me I used to be.
I let you change me
dim my light,
Take a part of me.

People will never see what I see
Never feel what I feel
I am in charge of my own happiness
No one can help me heal
I will.

I yearn for you.
However, it is not my intent.
I distance myself with purpose.

You are you.

I am me.

The illusion of ones
Feelings.

You brighten my moments.
You light up my mind.
You connect with my mental state
You give me a good vibe
I feel your energy
Radiating on to me
You seem to hold me on a pedestal
You value my time
You value me

I don't need anyone,
to entangle my emptions,
to fill me with empty potions,
I need someone who's genuine and honest.

I need someone who is...

someone who's strong when I am weak

who can see me when I don't see me

who can feel my energy

someone who can notice the small things

the list continues...

It is common,
to want a love so real, so strong

I want someone that doesn't say my list is too long.

I'm worth it.

Can I trust you?

Can I open up to you?

Can I let you know..

what causes me pain,

what causes my tears to fall,

and expect you to do the opposite?

I'm afraid of the fact that
I think of you when I wake up in the morning.

I've been picturing your face.
I've been thinking about...

As the petal is pressed
and the lights flash by
my thoughts are in distress
and the tears stream down
as I begin to realize,
you have the potential to mean a lot to me.
I have so much potential to care.
Honestly, I am scared,
Not because of you, but because of me.

I believe if I open up to you,
I'll be letting you in to my abyss.
However,
I don't know if I want you that deep

The last thing I wanted to do
was get close,
only because I still feel like there's
a hole.

But,
let me make a toast
to your mindset
to your growth
to the part of me that I didn't see
to the part of you that wanted me

You've officially attracted me,
not just to your physicality
but to your brain, your energy.
I'm shocked.
The one thing I thought I didn't need,
has been placed right before me,
but has been there all along
waiting in the back patiently

There's been a battle declared.
between my heart and my mind.

An important part of mental health is "SOLIDARITY"

The view of the sunset gave one great "SOLITUDE"

I need to be content with being alone.
Not necessarily being alone,
but being with myself
Not depending on anyone else
to make me happy
or to put a smile upon my face.

I am stronger than I think.

It's okay to not be okay,
to not want to interact with an entire population.

It's okay to sometimes sleep away the day.

It's okay to feel like your life is bad.

One day you will look back and
you will realize the lesson
you learned
from every situation

It's okay, you'll be okay one day.

I'll be okay one day.

Philippians 4:6

Don't worry about anything
but PRAY about everything.

With thankful hearts,
offer up your prayers
and requests
to GOD.

My heart is like an ocean.
Its waters run deep.
Its full of hidden treasures and mysteries

My heart is like a rose,
with beauty so sweet
and thorns that cut deep
to protect its most fragile parts.

You are beautiful with all your flaws.

Thank you for your energy.

Thank you for respecting my feelings and my sensitivity.

You are a very unique being.

Its light,
It shines.
Likewise to you, it radiates,
and its energy surrounds me.
Likewise to you, it's inevitable that I am surrounded by its rays of light
To me you are like the sun,
shining bright no matter how dim it may seem.
Even when covered by clouds, I still feel its heat, its energy.

However your flames are immense.
The closer I get, the more potential
It presents for me to overheat.
But the close proximity to you,
may remove some of the ice running through my blood stream.

Even if I am mine
and you are yours.

There's potential for me to overheat but you may remove some of the ice running through.

Now I know I may never have you in my grasp, but just like the sun..

It's a fight going on between myself and I.
I am fully aware
of the potential there is to grow.
However I am scared,
that my thoughts will overwhelm or overtake.

"The biggest lesson you can get is from yourself. Try to be a light."

-Dad

I am at stake
I need to be free
There's healing to do and the only one responsible for my healing is me.

John 8:32

And ye shall know the Truth
And the Truth shall set you free.

(Jesus speaking)

Love show your beauty through the darkness
Shine your light
You may be dimmer than the brightest
We feel your vibe
We see your tide

You are you

Not defined by a reflection

You are simply perfection

With your flaws that are not flaws

It's all perception

Love, show your beauty
even when darkness comes
and when the lights around you shine
shine bright

Shine your light as far as the eye can see.
You may be dimmer than the brightest
but your light is necessary

You are you
Not defined by a reflection
However, you are simply perfection
Even with your flaws that are not flaws

It's all perception.

The nice one
The one you look over
The one that you set boundaries for without hesitation

Not knowing that the one you're looking over is the one you want to see.

The way he makes you smile,
you can't explain.
The happiness he makes you feel
so genuine, so real, so soon.
You think to yourself is this to good to be true?
Is he filling your mind with empty promises and expectations?
Is he wasting your time..
but there's no waste in having a friend
for now,
knowing there's potential there.
One day..
Maybe not today but one day..
Maybe soon..
One day.

You may say I'm perfect,
although, I am far from
perfection.
However my love..
I see perfection in you.
You have no flaws in my eyes.
I accept you for you.
You are perfection to me.

Never did I ever think,
I'd fall into your arms and sink so deep.
Never did I think you'd catch me.
Will you catch me?
If I fall too deep..
if my love for you is felt so deep..
Will you drown in the waters with me?
Will you take the dive?
Will you go through this journey with me?
Would you stay by my side if I gave you the chance?
I guess we'll have to see
I guess you'll have to prove yourself to me.

You have to prove yourself to me only because,
I've been told so many sweet nothings
so, when you speak your sweet words
I can't always trust the words you speak.
I don't want to have expectations and get let down you see.
It's not you, it's me.
You came in to my life during a time
where my heart is not all the way healed.
I have to build myself up
for me
and maybe
potentially
for you.

Good things come to those who wait,
And those who wait gain better benefits in the long run.

Baby, take your time with me.
Baby, keep me at a good pace.
Know my limits, learn me.
Don't let my emotions cloud my mind or decisions.
Don't take advantage of my kindness
I'm fragile, I didn't say I'm weak.
I'm just easier to break at the moment. So you shouldn't say words that
cause harm to my feelings, to my heart.
Since you are aware of my vulnerable state,
you should not do things you tell me you won't do.
You shouldn't give me promises or speak empty words.
Be careful with me baby.

Your words are so soft spoken.
Your smile, so genuine.
Thank you for being you and speaking honest words out your lips
You gave me something I've never seen before.

I'm terrified,
I just want you to know.

I feel as if I have opened myself once again..
to the horrors of love and attachment.
There is always a chance of a happy ending..
however, there's a chance of a tragic ending, and a shattered heart.

I love you
and when I say these three words
I mean them so sincerely
so dearly, because
I do.

I never believed my heart
would open up so wide.
I didn't think my bloodstream
could run through another's tide
but it does.

You light my world up.
You light up my life.
You keep me grounded.
You brighten my nights.
My sunshine.

I look upon your eyes and see,
so much behind the gleam.
As my hands run down your skin
my heartbeat tends to increase.
When our eyes meet I can,
hardly speak, hardly breathe.
You take my breathe away
I thank God for blessing me with you
because he made you for me.
I owe him everything
for a blessing so sweet,
for a love so kind,
for the answers to my prayers
for giving me everything that I need.

Philippians: 4:19

*The same GOD who takes care of me
will supply all your needs from his glorious riches which have been
given to us in CHRIST JESUS.*

You've presented me with a love
so kind so sweet.
There hasn't been any wasted time,
every moment with you,
has been a meaningful moment.
Every word you speak holds value
because you value me.
You value my mind.
You looked past the physical aspect,
and when you looked in my eyes
you wanted to see what was behind,
never before seen.
The mystery waiting to be dissected.

My heart was neglected,
like the old book on the shelf.
However you picked me up and wanted to read my pages.
Took me a part piece by piece
and in return to what's beyond the binding,
You've presented me with a love
so kind, so sweet.

1st John 4:10

This is real love

Letter to my Sunflower in the Rain.

Baby I love you,
and this love is what it seems
it can't be cut from the seams.
When I speak these words to you
they are not empty,
but full of life and light.
The light that you bring into my life.
This love doesn't not make me fight
It makes me scream, for more, for more of what you bring.
I yearn for you,
your spirit, your energy.
The way you complement me.
You were not the missing piece
you were the blessing,
made for me and I see.

So when I speak these three words to you,
know I mean them from the deepest parts of me.
I have felt this love for you
when the thought of you was just a
figment of my dreams.
I didn't know that you would be the angel
sent for me
to keep me at peace.
When GOD said
"He is the one but you have to allow him to be."
I felt those words through my blood stream.
Baby, I love you.

-Poodah

As I sit here staring out,
I see the empty tree branches
the full bushes on the ground
the leaves have already been swept by the wind ..
so there is really no sound
but there is a presence of peace.
A peace that is so necessary to receive.
I almost want to reach out and hold on to it you see.
Hoping that it consumes my being
and places itself permanently
so I could accept it with open arms
wholeheartedly
Peace is what I yearn for
what I seek.

Philippians 4:7

And the peace of GOD,
which transcends all understanding,
will guard your hearts and your minds
in CHRIST JESUS.

Philippians 4:7

And the peace of GOD,
which transcends all understanding,
will guard your hearts and your minds
in CHRIST JESUS.

<u>Words from the Author</u>

I want to encourage each of you to keep breaking barriers and chasing your dreams from now on until the end of time because this life is not what It seems,

it tries to break you down piece by piece, but you have to keep your head up you see, your downfall can only be your downfall if you allow it to be. Life will try to bring you down when you're at your highest, when your light is shining the brightest, people will try to dim your light, your shine. In my life I've made the decision to shine, I will shine with or without another presence,

I will shine, and there is only one crime I can commit against myself which is dimming my light for another flame that doesn't burn as bright. I want to formally introduce myself, my name is De'sha Monet Anthony, I'm from Long Beach, California. I am currently 20 years old, I graduated high school at 16, and I will be graduating with a Bachelor's Degree in Human Resource Management and a minor in Psychology in December of 2020. I am a proud member of Alpha Kappa Alpha Sorority, Inc, the first Greek sorority founded by black women on January 15, 1908. I have plans to start non-profit organizations after I graduate my goal is to become a successful entrepreneur that is able to shine light and make an impact. When I say things out loud, sometimes they sound impossible to reach, however impossible is my peak,

don't ever let anyone put limitations on what you can achieve, because as I said before, this life is not what it seems,

this life is what you make it, make it all that it can be, this put together person wasn't always me.. this put together person wasn't always me.

At 11 years old, my happy family broke, I found out that my parents were getting a divorce, they were separating.

I felt like I was loosing my family, I felt like I lost me. I developed an eating disorder, I was sinking, in depression, I was sinking and then we moved back to Cali.

At 12 years old I was raped by my dad's best-friend, a person we trusted, a person we knew, I knew the depth of what just happened, to speak up? I couldn't pursue, I held that secret in for 6 years.. It was the hardest thing I'd ever had to do. Too protect the ones I loved... I forgot about me.. don't ever forget about you, I was depressed, I developed PTSD, I went through a period of self-harm. I didn't take care of me, always take care of you. I'm telling you all this to show you that though all this happened I still got through. My breaking point didn't break me. I kept pushing. At 13 I made the decision that I'd graduate early from high school. At 16 I graduated from high school and attended college in the fall, at 17 I was diagnosed with systemic lupus, a chronic auto immune disease. I already showed symptoms, now there was a label with a stigma attached, for all the things wrong with me. I've went through a lot, there have been times when I didn't want to live anymore, my heart was so low, sinking beneath the floor, but I kept my head up, my crown didn't fall, and I wouldn't be here today if God wasn't there through it all...

Today I would like to pass the torch, I pass on the light,
I pass on some strength, I challenge each of you to always fight... until the end, fight for what you believe in, fight for what's right, fight for your dreams, achieve your goals, no matter what life throws at you because this life is not what it seems. You can get through anything you're stronger than you think.
Remember to always try to reach the highest peak
and keep in mind that your downfall is only your downfall if you allow it to be.

Shine your light.